Christopher Prewitt

PARADISE HAMMER

SurVision Books

First published in 2018 by
SurVision Books
Dublin, Ireland
www.survisionmagazine.com

Copyright © Christopher Prewitt, 2018

Cover photograph: "Der Nagel" by Günther Uecker, Düsseldorf
Design © SurVision Books, 2018

ISBN: 978-1-9995903-9-0

This book is in copyright. No part of this publication may be reproduced, stored in a retrieval system or transmitted in any form or by any means without the prior permission in writing from the publisher.

For Jeffrey and Kim

Acknowledgements

Grateful acknowledgement is made to the editors of the following, in which a number of these poems, or versions of them, originally appeared:

antinarrative journal: "Milk Money"
Bloodroot: "Dry Skin and Morning"
Eunoia Review: "42 Girls Auditioned"
Fried Chicken and Coffee: "Kentucky Sonnet"
Merida Review: "Moonlight on Meat-Eating Plants," "Public Relations"
SurVision Magazine: "Blue Assemblage with a Horse," "Friday Afternoon as Spiritual Autobiography," "Threnody"

CONTENTS

Public Relations	4
Friday Afternoon as Spiritual Autobiography	6
Red Jesus	8
Floodlight Sonata	9
Moonlight on Meat-Eating Plants	10
Christ Tulips among the Bleeding Fungus: Two Eclogues	12
Kentucky Sonnet	15
42 Girls Auditioned	16
Threnody	18
Poema with Two Ghosts and a Wall	20
Four Equally Viable Philosophies	21
Milk Money	22
Poema with Glaucoma, Anxiety, and a Saturday Morning	24
Floating on Graduation Day	26
Poema for James Tate	27
21st Century West Virginia Blues	28
Saint Monica	30
La Vaca	31
Just to Clarify	32
Dry Skin and Morning	34
Blue Assemblage with a Horse	36

Public Relations

It has been raining
but only on that side of town.

I go in my quiet way
nursing a fire ball,

wanting to be held in the air
that is screaming at me,

signing in at the front desk
of an old building

stained with streaks of milk
on the windows.

A young woman in a black dress
comes from the back to take my coat

and my teeth.
I try to ask her

why do daughters inflict violence on one another,
but she's already at work

on my tongue.
It's a device

that was once bright
as the silver coins

Judas has claimed as his Forever.
There's no time

to think about the rust.
I have to go.

I have to sit at my desk.
I have to write something brief

and apologetic
on behalf of my top floor shadow,

spinning with gold in his lap
and blood on his cheeks,

the company president.

Friday Afternoon as Spiritual Autobiography

I have driven a nail
through an orchid.
I think of you,

Saint Augustine,
gathering fruit
for your false priest,

as your mother floats
above you.
Now my face has left my face.

Though I am firmly planted
in the Midwest like a corporation,
I want to sing hymns

to milk and forget I was ever lost
in the woods, guided by syringe
eyed children.

That was so long ago,
but I am still a little boy
sitting in my mother's bathtub

with my broken leg,
and my mother in hysterics
on the phone

trying to find someone with a car
to drive us to the hospital.

I don't ask my face where it's going,
it's somewhere strange
and beautiful.

If you should find my eyes,
O my love,
don't cover them.

Red Jesus

Red Jesus,
O Red Jesus,
rising through the trees and above the mountains,
give me back my eyes.
I can feel as I know you do
the animal turning in my spine.

Sweet Red Jesus,
if you had kissed me
when we were both apprentices
under a summer storm,
I would have let you
place your true red hand
on the nesting red owl of my breast.

You know where
I'm driving to in a hurry.
You know why I'm laughing.
There is the manifesto
written by the ants
and we all know it by heart,
Red Jesus.
It's that you think you can
frighten me by appearing
unannounced
at 6:00 am.

Sweet baby,
your pocketknife doesn't scare me.

Floodlight Sonata

You know the death mother,
her pale face, her trembling hands,
her ways: Love only

the black angel
rising from your head,
she says with her eyes

to gray waters.
Impossible!
For one does not live

among powerlines and locomotives
without pressing their lips
against the naked heart pounding in the vegetation.

And so I say: My love,
into a floating music that is yellow
where there is cool water and sweet berries,

I know my mouth will
with your mouth get there.
Into you only it is possible,

the long awaited dissolution
of 5:00 pm, of the storm drain,
of the parking meters.

Moonlight on Meat-Eating Plants

Here's how I write poems.
I live in a town.
I open my mouth.
The first person to kiss me
I come to resent.
The first gentle rain
to sleep at my feet
I hand over to the authorities.
Anyone who dines with me
at a Waffle House or a Golden Corral
has a friend for life.
Anyone who writes poems and hates poems
containing more than one language
and/or positive feelings
toward chain family restaurants
might as well kiss me
con lengua y uñas.
At the end of a long day being no one,
I make a simple dinner
for my wife,
and then I rub her back
until she falls asleep.
Just as I'm about to fall asleep,
I take my 3 subject notebook
and mechanical pencil
from the floor.

Every night I write
these same 2 lines over and over:

> I am an avalanche of roses,
> I am a full-throated nativity science.

I can't keep my eyes open.
I never get the title right.

Christ Tulips among the Bleeding Fungus: Two Eclogues

I.

In the colorless and burning puritan
rain, I pull my eyes behind my head.

In this perpetual mildewed 12 month winter,
I rename myself Headache Factory.

On this side of the Ohio River,
all the food tastes like empty stadiums

with a riot squad outside,
and you come home on the verge of tears

like a delinquent recurring payment.
All this rain but bone dry is the pavement

that leads me to your trembling hands.
Come on, come on—

with these delicate treasures that run
marble countertops with chemicals and dark green rags,

touch me.
With these soft windchimes painted red

at the tips like a row of honest hearses,
touch me.

II.

Oh, my love,
no more than an Eastern Phoebe

do I wish
to be American.

My suitcase is packed
with my eyelids

for the summer.
If I fall asleep on your naked

bedroom floor,
do not permit even the Canadian snow to fall

on me.

(Only you, please

fall on me, across me, over me
bend as Pauline was bade to by Robert Browning.

Or hell,
my cheek is on the table.

I'd rather feel you
rubbing your vanilla sun-

soaked blank
into my starless parenthesis

before the end of Christ's surveillance.)
Now everything is coral:

accordions and cameras,
empty bird cages and fire

hydrants, breast to
breast, mouth to mouth,

I am only yours
in never-ending coral.

Kentucky Sonnet

Limping with my dead man and my mountain beyond the moonlit
  bell tower
Limping with my dead man and my mountain beyond the road that
  ends at a mountain

I come to know my body
prepared to lose everything

Father if I wore your blue suit to your funeral
I don't remember

I held strange women with dark hair
sucking the roots of a sugar maple

I held catholic ideas and nude irises
drowning in the milk of a star that I commanded

my mouth dark with dirt
my small ruby, your broken son's head foaming and turning in the
  backseat of your Cadillac

held in the heart of a hornet's nest
am I someone you'd choose to know?

42 Girls Auditioned

Holy cow, I was cast
as an extra in a sitcom.
I get to wear purple

bicycle shorts, my
face gets to say, This
is extraordinary news

you're telling me
in this metropolitan
coffee shop, but not

the kind of news I
should be audible about.
I'm so excited, I'm

telling everyone I meet
while I can still talk
and keep my brown bangs.

And do you know what
else? I downloaded this
killer app to my white rose.

I get to stand by
the ash where my high school
sweetheart burned, and

I can hear his final words
whenever I want with this
rose. Everything good is

happening at once so suddenly
for me, it's easy to forget
sometimes these days how

horrible I feel pretending
I can ride a bicycle
made of fire. And then

there's the sound of choking
and tears and he's gone,
but I'm sure that like

all the other girls, he's really
happy for me that I've made
it this far.

Threnody

The old men enter the white barn.
They leave

in fitted white tuxedos.
Everything turns pink

after you rain.
The cow blinking away a fly in the tall grass

was a starved calf last spring.
The stains are fresh

in the air,
some are gray and some are black

perpetually above the New River Valley
in southern Virginia.

I am turning back
into an egg   I remember

when my baby brother
had his turn

on his messy bed in the summer.
Later that night my hair was wet

in my mother's white tub,
and I cried

because of the things I'd said.
In the dry winter

she gave birth to him all over again.
I kissed him on his red face

all over again I am born
gripping my cracking mottled stone.

Poema with Two Ghosts and a Wall

Eating the soup the color of the rain.
The man and his face to the wall.
This is the wall; its color is red.
His fingers turn gray

when touching the body
of the gray horse
that comes and goes
comes and goes

like the desire to be born again
in the red wall.

I've been there before
but I am fine being dead,
puckering my lips at the man with his face to the wall,
eating the soup the color of rain.

Four Equally Viable Philosophies

1. No good ever came of poets.

2. No good ever came of poets
   pushing in their eyes and teeth.

3. No good ever came of poets
   pushing in their eyes and teeth
   to activate a holy father machine.

4. Who doesn't want **G O D** to be a machine
   that we placed in the air
   that when you get low you can plug yourself in

   you you little knot of shrieking rattlesnakes

   you just plug yourself into a wall
   the machine feels you
   feels it all   the machine
   sucks the black jelly beans
   out of your skull.

Milk Money

Like a pair of dead roses
let's sing in the park.

When Gretta finds us,
she will put us in a white vase

no matter how dark
our singing.

I don't know about you,
but I adore Gretta.

When she goes to the hospital,
I paint portraits of her in oil

on paper plates.
I tape them to green waves

in the lake on Falcone's private
land. It's his money and dread,

he can be an abomination
if he wants, for there's money enough

to silence god
and his god, too.

As for you, my best friend,
with your open mouth

a dandelion
rendered in purple pastel,

not tonight.

Poema with Glaucoma, Anxiety, and a Saturday Morning

The world is closing in on me.

I know, I know: I'm not the only one
who feels like Orpheus

crossing the Ohio River for love,
crossing a muted rose
metal bridge
when the cloudless blue sky is hazy,
and the new dark's coming on.

Things being the way they are, ostensibly religious
public celebrations of the phallus,
and how my eyes convey to me the material world,
ain't what they used to be.

First, I noticed it with you,
the sky's new hazy blue and the dark, when we were
standing outside St. Louis Cathedral in New Orleans, Louisiana.

I felt sick at the aquarium. I tried to meditate on the plane.

"The key is to accept the vibrancy of all things,"
says the bird that resides in the mouth
of the pointillism girl.

Okay. Alright.

Even if you have to work on a Saturday morning
while everyone else is painting watercolors of the open mouth and
the sharp teeth at the tailgate,
and the collective mind goes to the
When is this all gonna be over—Soon? song?

Hell yes.

When a dog small enough to be a rat approaches,
slightly confused but obviously happy,

and someone opens her umbrella
as small worms the color of Monday fall from the black above her
brown hair.

"Not a cloud in the sky," the worms sing,
and everyone laughs.

Floating on Graduation Day

A cloud passed overhead.
My desk was below me.
The school was below my desk.

Nobody seemed to notice me,
this orange pink thing laughing in the air.

But there was nothing to laugh about.

Entering the bosom of the cloud,
I felt as if I had something in my eye.

A footstep at first. Then a thousand.

Then it dawned on me.
I was the mother of sidewalks.

Poema for James Tate

I was thinking about my friend Arthur,
recently deceased, and I started to cry.
The tears were powerful. Physicists
in cowboy hats would hoot and dream
at such power. "Hey, fella, watch it
with that weed whacker, will you?" the grass
cried out. "I'm sorry," I said.
"I have the soul of a poet, so I cry
sometimes at the thought of things."
"Well, keep it steady." It had rained hard
the previous night, and it looked as though
the plains were moments away from leftovers.
I remembered a turkey ruben from
my childhood. My lip quivered and I looked
into the oncoming rain. "Jesus, what now?" the grass
yelled. But not so much as the word turkey
would leave my mouth, salty with tears.
"Ah, the hell with this," the grass said
and dislodged itself from the ground.
Into the air and away it went.
Somehow like a mother bird
I held myself together.

21st Century West Virginia Blues

A black sun
nauseated
above Huntington.

I know
today
will be the same as
yesterday.

O God
come
and spit
on me.

My eyes are closed.
My animal leads me
outside
before the dawn.

The broken parking meters,
the snow

above my knees,
and the smell of burning
plastic,

the same
opioid
stain.

Who is made of light
and able
to defy
the crooked master?
Who is able to resist

kissing
the chain
master's chains?

I know
today
will be the same as
yesterday.

Saint Monica

It is a dull light
that guides Saint Monica
through the night sky.

Forever her sharp teeth
cut through dark clouds.
Lightning cannot wound her
blue scales and gold fins.

Look out your window
on a quiet evening, my child.

See that it is not
the body of Christ
upon her purple tongue,

but your shadow
growing larger.

La Vaca

The baby wants to eat
red meat from la vaca's mouth

The baby says the glass
tasted better in the sky

The baby, oh the baby,
they said, is a miracle

The baby is a 42-year-old eunuch named Kevin
who is getting a stained-glass haircut

who is riding a convulsing burro
into the mountainous parlor of the dead moon

never to be seen again
without an open mouth or eyes full of wonder

for everything's understood

At last the winter's over
O mi vaca, come join me in the sun.

Just to Clarify

This is a ghost
disguised as a book.

What you think are poems
are boxcutters.

Jocasta knew, Gertrude, too,
why everything was falling apart

at once around them.
Whoever coined the term

coined the term,
probably never saw a cent.

Saint Monica,
in the naked branches of the frozen tree,

the dead man laughing
is my father.

To a corporation
anyone who doesn't sit

on the Board
is an adjunct

full of screaming roses.
This is why so many of us must sleep

with constant white noise.
Saint Monica,

you prayed and became a god-
sized angler fish.

It is often broken glass when I sing of summer.
I sound better singing in a box fan.

Dry Skin and Morning

I am trying to sleep
in the warm cab
of my father's truck

But soon the school bus
that single red-breasted
Medusa
with screaming hair
will come

for me
and my baby
brother

I slept
but I didn't dream
last night

Sometimes I am
soft and constant rain
above winter trees
sometimes
I am a woman
gathering lavender
for a girl a niece
I think

stepping off a train
but then I wake up
with a sore throat
in the place where
the dream was

Sometimes as he leaves us
parked at the edge
of the road
to feed the cows
I notice the blood

on my father's hands
but now the bus has come
and we must board
like weak fire
with dirty coins
under our tongues.

Blue Assemblage with a Horse

This blue night expels its white horse
through my bedroom window.
Along the hillside the pink and yellow houses
marinating in winter moonlight,
and slowly and not slowly

all the warm places decay.
At first I didn't like myself
standing at the end of the checkered hallway
with my dented brass and sheet music.
You made me turn a funny color,

I couldn't breathe when you looked at me,
and when you looked at me
how easily my jaw broke off,
just a solitary look from you
in your blue doorway

and it was like the wind
passing through the web of a twilight spider.
The earth manages a full rotation.
There is humming and the whistling of steam.
What a strange, beautiful machine

you've asked me to set my teeth upon,
O sexless mover of the priest
that floats above my bed,
your four legs kicking,
your bright white hooves.

More poetry published by SurVision Books

Noelle Kocot. Humanity
(New Poetics: USA)
ISBN 978-1-9995903-0-7

Ciaran O'Driscoll. The Speaking Trees
(New Poetics: Ireland)
ISBN 978-1-9995903-1-4

Elin O'Hara Slavick. Cameramouth
(New Poetics: USA)
ISBN 978-1-9995903-4-5

Anatoly Kudryavitsky. Stowaway
(New Poetics: Ireland)
ISBN 978-1-9995903-2-1

George Kalamaras. That Moment of Wept
ISBN 978-1-9995903-7-6

Anton G. Leitner. Selected Poems 1981–2015
Translated from German
ISBN 978-1-9995903-8-3

Sergey Biryukov. Transformations
Translated from Russian
(New Poetics: Russia)
ISBN 978-1-9995903-5-2

Maria Grazia Calandrone. Fossils
Translated from Italian
(New Poetics: Italy)
ISBN 978-1-9995903-6-9

Our books are available to order via
http://survisionmagazine.com/books.htm

www.ingramcontent.com/pod-product-compliance
Lightning Source LLC
Chambersburg PA
CBHW061313040426
42444CB00010B/2610